God's Vision in a Dɪ

Michelle Creary

PROTECTIVE HANDS
Communications

Riviera Beach, FL

ISBN 978-0-9892028-8-6

Library of Congress Control Number: 2013946190

Published by Protective Hands Communications
Riviera Beach, FL 33404
Toll free: 866-457-1203
www.protectivehands.com
Email: info@protectivehands.com

Printed in the United States of America

CONTENTS

Dedication

This book is dedicated to my Lord and Savior Jesus Christ, who is the Shepherd of my daily journey to eternal life with Him! It is by faith in Him why you hold this book in your hands. I give Him all the honor and glory for all things in my life.

Acknowledgements

A special thanks to my husband and confidant, Mr. Bryon Creary, for all his love, support and talent in executing the illustrations for this book under the guidance of the Holy Spirit.

I would also like to thank our children, Abigail, Brianna, Chloe, Daniel and Emilee for keeping us inspired.

To my parents Emanuel and Petrona Clarke, my sisters, Maxine and Marsha, my brother, Maurice and their families. To my readers, may God bless you and enrich your vision of Him in glory, awaiting that day when He shall unite with those of us who have lived for Him.

"I will stand upon my watch, and set me upon the tower, and will watch to see what he will say unto me, and what I shall answer when I am reproved. And the Lord answered me, and said, Write the vision, and make it plain upon tables, that he may run that readeth it. For the vision is yet for an appointed time, but at the end it shall speak, and not lie: though it tarry, wait for it: because it will surely come, it will not tarry.

Habakkuk 2:1-3

Introduction

Seven dreams, seven interpretations from God, seven years later! Finally God's will for this book is manifested in its fullness. It's been a journey, but by the grace of God, I am still leaning on His everlasting arms. Seven years ago as I was intensely seeking who God really was in my life. I started to have some meaningful, repetitive and sequential dreams. These dreams were such that I still remember the detail of each one and their interpretations.

I remember going into days of fasting and prayer, asking the Lord to give me the meaning of each dream. Finally one day while I was at work the Lord started to minister to me about the dreams and their meaning. I started to write down everything He was telling me.

Seven years later, as a more mature child of God, I was looking through some paperwork and I found, "God's Vision In A Dream," the title to the book that He had instructed me to write.

The Lord Jesus commanded me to write what I'd seen and heard in my dreams. He was specific in His instructions for the book. He told me to write a simple, easy to understand book so that even a young child could read and understand the message He is sending to His people. God wants me to tell His people that He loves us all and that His greatest vision and aspiration is for mankind to make the choice to live for Him here on earth, so that we can enjoy eternal life in His presence one day. God has prepared a place far better than earth for all who sacrifice and live a Christ-like life for Him here on earth. He is coming back soon and it is His vision of preparation for us that He has given to me in these dreams.

The Journey

As I entered into a night vision (dream) by the Holy Spirit of God, I found myself walking on a paved road. This road was very straight, I could actually see the end of it. The road was also very narrow and paved with white stones. On the left side of the road were diverse and countless fruit trees. I had never seen fruits so rich in color and so beautifully groomed, as these fruits appeared to be. As I continued walking, deep inside, I knew there was a destination to reach, although I did not know where that destination would be.

Half way into my journey the Holy Spirit revealed two things to me. First of all, I was not allowed to pick and eat from the trees until I reached my destination. Secondly, the Holy Spirit disclosed the name of my destination in a language that was unknown to me.

As I walked along this narrow road, I saw a man walking towards me. I stopped and asked him for directions to my destination. Without saying a word he pointed in the direction that he was coming from. His countenance was bright and happy as he enjoyed eating the fruit in his hands. Just as I was about to pick some fruit from one of the trees, a voice commanded me not to.

I continued on my journey and before long I arrived at a small slope. Immediately ahead of me was the most magnificent sight I'd ever seen. The destination that I so desperately longed to reach had led me to a beautiful snow white church with a steeple and a huge cross on top of it. This beautiful church was sitting in the midst of a beautifully landscaped area with green grass. It was a peaceful place overlooking the entire world. From where I was standing, I could see endless rays of lights throughout the world. There was complete peace upon the world.

Upon arriving at the church, I began to praise the Lord for helping me through my long journey and for the beauty I saw in front of me. As I was worshipping the Lord, He spoke to me. "Congratulations," He said. "You have overcome, now rejoice in the spirit and enjoy your portion of the tree of life."

With the anointing of the Spirit of God upon me, I began to skip and dance, rejoicing in the presence of the Lord.

3

After sometime, I started down the same road I had just travelled, rejoicing in the spirit of the Lord as I walked. But there was something different about the road this time. Instead of a stony pavement, I was on a road that looked like glass or gold. As I was skipping along the road, the Lord told me that it was now okay for me to pick and eat as much fruit as I desired from the trees.

Interpretation of The Journey

The Narrow White Stony Paved Road

This road represents the way in which those who choose to follow Me must walk continuously. This is the way of righteousness and it is the only way to eternal life. At times your way may seem foggy and gloomy, but keep on walking towards your heavenly promise because you walk by faith and not by sight (2 Corinthians 5: 7). Remember that I have given you My Spirit, therefore I Am always with you. Keep on walking in obedience to Me for your reward is with Me and I have prepared a glorious place for all My people who diligently live for Me.

Bible references

Matthews 7:14 "Because strait is the gate, and narrow is the way which leadeth unto life, and few there be that find it."

John 14: 2 "In my father's house are many mansions: If it were not so I would have told you. I go to prepare a place for you."

The Beautiful and Enticing Fruit Trees

The presence of the fruit trees signifies two things. First, the joy felt in seeing the beauty in all the trees signifies the peace and blessings I have promised to all who labor for Me on earth.

However, the temptation of the delicious fruit from the trees signifies the trials and tests that those who follow Me shall face as they journey through this life. My elect shall endure to the end, because I have promised to always be there to direct your steps.

Look with your spiritual eyes and see beyond this world. See the beautiful place that I have prepared for all those who overcome. Cheer up and hold on faithfully to Me, for you will eat from the tree of life forevermore. Remember that when you are faced with hard times there is always hope for a better day through Me.

Bible reference

Hebrew 13vs5 "…….I will never leave thee, nor forsake thee."

The White Church

The church represents a body of people that I will return for and they will inherit the

Kingdom of heaven forever. My people must be spotless and blameless, a holy nation. My people must be righteous and to them will be given the power to judge and rule the world.

Holiness and purity of heart are absolute requirements to inherit the Kingdom of God. I love you so much that I have provided a way to achieve your goal of righteousness. I left you the blueprints of godly characteristics, these virtues are the fruits of the Spirit (Galatians 5).

See that you pray fervently to Me so that you may possess these virtues which comes only from Me. You have all been given free access to Me through your repentance. I am merciful. Ask Me to forgive you and I will. So make use of My mercy now, for when I return, I will come to judge.

Bible reference

Ephesians 5:27: "He might present it to himself a glorious church, not having spot or wrinkle or any such thing, but that it should be holy and without blemish."

1Peter 1:16: "Be he holy for I am holy."

Psalm 96:13: " For He cometh to judge the earth, He shall judge the world with righteousness and judge His people with His truth".

Revelation 2:26 "And he that overcometh, and keepeth my works unto the end, to him will I give power over the nations."

The Delicious Fruits

The tasty fruits represents both earthly blessings and heavenly inheritance that I have promised to the righteous and to those who endure the journey in this life. Hold on to My promises for I have declared in My words, "that the eye hath not seen nor ear heard, neither have entered into the heart of man, the things which God hath prepared for them that love Him." (1 Corinthians 2:9). Keep My commandments and you will be blessed abundantly in this life and the life to come.

Bible reference

Revelation 2:7 "....To him that overcometh will I give to eat of the tree of life, which is in the midst of the paradise of God."

Paradise

I found myself swimming to shore, only to discover that I had been the only survivor of a plane crash. When I got to the seashore, I realized I had entered into a war zone. I started to walk towards an area where I saw a nun and a man talking. The nun was Mother Theresa, a person I had only heard about since her passing. She was known for her passion for helping others and a life solely devoted to God. I felt secure as I walked toward her. I told her that I was trying to find my way home.

I was still in a state of shock, but Mother Teresa immediately knew where home was for me. She called a man and spoke to him in another language that only the two of them could understand. I could tell by their demeanor that she had instructed him to take me to a safe place.

Instantly, he took hold of my hand and proceeded down the road. This road was dark and narrow, but more evident was the sound of bombs going off all around us.

Naturally I started to feel fearful, but when I looked at the man's face, I saw no fear. All the commotion around him did not phase him, which gave me confidence to keep on going. Moreover, even though the road was pitch black, I could see a soft, but very bright light in the far distance. As we walked, the Spirit of God in me as well as the presence of the man kept me comforted and at peace.

While I was walking, the Holy spirit spoke to me with a comforting voice and told me that everything would be alright. He told me not to be afraid. The Lord also told me that I was going to die, but I was to remain bold because I would not feel the pain of death. As we continued towards the light, I realized the light was getting closer and brighter to us. The man told me we were almost there. Wherever "there" was, I didn't know.

Suddenly, I saw a tall young man approaching. I quickly snatched my hand from the man leading me. Instinctively the man grabbed my hand and told me to never let go. Within moments of reaching our destination, the Spirit of God told me to turn around. To my surprise, standing behind us was the same tall young man with a weapon pointed directly at me. As I turned to look, the man leading me disappeared. The amazing thing was that even though he was not there physically, spiritually I could feel him still holding my hand.

13

The Holy spirit whispered to me and said, "Don't be afraid. Be brave for I will be with you unto death." With that reassurance, I lifted up my hands to heaven and asked God to receive me in His presence. I could feel no pain as I fell to the ground.

I perceived in my spirit that time had passed of which I could not account for. I saw my body as I struggled to stand to my feet. Something was definitely different and obvious. I had a new body, because there were no wounds. I was standing in the same light that I was walking towards earlier. I saw an area to my left and there stood a little girl and a woman. The little girl yelled to the woman. "That's the lady we were waiting on," she said. I was unaware of what she was talking about, nevertheless, they ran over to me and offered to take me home.

It seemed as if they too knew where home was for me, because I had no idea what was going on. Before long they took me in front of a huge golden gate, which looked heavenly and beautiful. They told me I had to enter through the gate alone.

As soon as I entered through the gate I was changed into new apparel. I was dressed in pure white. The sights were magnificent, marvelous, glorious and unbelievable. Words cannot describe what I saw and the peace I felt as I entered through the gate. Everyone there was dressed in pure white clothing. I saw men, women and children all worshipping

God on one accord. There was a choir of many people singing melodiously as numerous musicians played all types of instruments. An angel took me by the hand and led me to a place where I was told to relax and receive my reward. There were people resembling angels that were pampering and ministering to all the saints. I sat with gratitude, basking in the beauty of the atmosphere. There was fruits, flowers and music all around me. Some were talking about how beautiful it was. I heard the voice of an angelic being saying, "You are in paradise." The atmosphere of this place was gloriously filled with singing and the worship of God.

Interpretation: Paradise

The Presence Of War:

The presence of war represents the turmoil between nations and kingdoms promised to this generation. This must take place before I come, but those who are holy, peace will be given.

Bible reference

Matthew 24:7 - For nation shall rise against nation, kingdom against kingdom: and there shall be famines, and pestilence, and earthquakes, in divers places.

The Narrow Road:

Those who love Me must live a Godly life. My people will at times encounter adversities, but don't be afraid. Be powerful, be courageous; stand on My words. Stay close to Me and I will lead you into everlasting life. Death through Me is the gateway to life in paradise with Me forever.

Bible reference

Isaiah 25:8 - He will swallow up death in victory; and the tears from off all faces; and the rebuke of His people shall He take away from off all the earth: for the Lord hath spoken it.

The New Body:

To those who follow Me and endures this life I have promised a new body. You will not remember the hurt and pain of this life, but you will experience the fullness of My presence.

Bible reference

1Corinthians15: 44-45 - It is sown a natural body; it is raised a spiritual body. There is a natural body, and there is a spiritual body. And so it is written, the first man Adam was made a living soul; and the last Adam was made a quickening spirit.

Home:

For those who overcome, I have prepared a place for you. A place where I will be with you and you will be in My rest forever.

Bible reference

Luke 23:43 And Jesus said unto him, verily I say unto thee, today shalt thou be with me in paradise.

When The Saints Go Marching

I found myself among a multitude of people marching, singing and dancing with timbrels. We were marching on a straight and narrow road. As I looked ahead, I saw a beautiful iron gate leading into a place. I could not see what was beyond the gate, however I saw two angelic beings conducting a checkpoint. It was obvious that some type of criteria had to be met before anyone could enter. Some people were being rejected, while some were allowed through after the men at the gate examined them thoroughly. I suspected that some were afraid of what would happen to them when they got to the gate. In other words, they were singing and marching, but they had no confidence in their outcome. On the other hand, a great number of us were rejoicing and praising our God in confidence the closer we got to the checkpoint.

22

Not long after, a particular group of us arrived at the gate and to our astonishment, the angels immediately dropped their weapons and stood at attention saluting us as we entered through the gate.

Right away we entered into the most beautiful garden. It was a place of total peace and serenity. The flowers were so rich in color, they were moving with life. Everyone who entered into the garden was dancing, singing and worshipping God on one accord. It was as if we knew each other for a lifetime.

24

Interpretation: When The Saints Go Marching

The Multitude Of People:

Represented are all who were called into Christianity. Everyone who was conceived in this life has a purpose for My kingdom. I have created My people to first worship Me and second to labor in soul winning for My kingdom. I am always calling upon you. Some ignore My call and some answer, but all are called.

Listen carefully, for those who answer My call, I have a job for each of you to do here on earth. You were elected into the kingdom of God to achieve a particular task and on the final day your work will be evaluated; pass or fail.

So make your election sure by seeking the will of God for yourself. In other words, ask Me, *"Lord what do you want me to do for the building of your kingdom?"* I will answer you and your responsibility is to act upon My answer.

The parable about the men and their talents in Matthew 25 is to remind you that many are called, but few are chosen. The key to being chosen is to follow My leadership, meaning let Me lead and you follow.

The Rejects:

The rejected are brethren who are preaching, teaching, dancing and singing among the multitude of My children, but are not doing it sincerely from their hearts. They are not worshipping Me because they love Me, instead they are going through the motions to obtain the praise of men. Therefore, they are so-called Christians, full of uncertainty and fear in their hearts. There are those who have answered my call to Christianity, but for them it stopped there. They have not set My will as the first priority in their life. They have not done what I have elected them to do for the kingdom of God. They have not sown a spiritual seed in the ears of a sinner, they have not helped each other nor have they loved each other with a sincere and pure heart. These are the ones I will turn from Me and cast into outer darkness, they are the rejects.

Bible reference

Matthew 7:21 - Not everyone that saith unto me Lord, Lord shall enter into the kingdom of heaven; but he that doeth the will of my father which is in heaven.

The Overcomers:

My children will march, dance and sing with confidence and hope in what I have prepared for them beyond the gate, which is everlasting life in paradise. Those who make it through the gate have done My will and shall reap an inheritance promised to all who endure. You will overcome only when you obey Me. For an Overcomer is a disciple of Jesus who endures the spiritual race with faith and hope to see that which he or she have believed in, become reality. ETERNAL LIFE!

Not all called will be chosen because of disobedience to Me. So, if you are having a problem with obeying the will of God, pray and ask your Father in heaven to strengthen you in deciphering His will for your life as a Christian so you may possess the spirit of obedience. Furthermore ask Him for boldness to do that which He commands you to do. In that way you will not live as a so-called believer, but you will be a laboring believer for the Kingdom of the Most High God. Not all will make it through those pearly white gates of heaven on the final day of judgment, only those who do the will of God.

Bible reference

Revelation 3:12 - Him that overcometh will I make a pillar in the temple of my God, and he shall go no more out: and I will write upon him the name of my God, and the name of the city of my God, which is New Jerusalem, which cometh down out of heaven from my God: and I will write upon him my new name.

Streets of Gold and Tree of Life

I found myself standing somewhere I had never been before. The atmosphere was different, it was totally peaceful and the energy was so strong, it was as if one single divine force was in control. There was an unexplainable bright light that filled the atmosphere, more splendid than the sun and the moon. I noticed that I was standing on a road, but its reflection was that of a clear piece of ice. There was something supernatural and spectacular about where I was in this dream, so I paid closer attention to its detail.

This road was filled with pure gold and reflected like clear glass. As I stood there I noticed an unusual and beautiful tree possessing twelve different kinds of fruit. I had never seen such beauty.

The Spirit of God immediately told me that this tree was the tree of life promised to all who endures the spiritual race to the end. There was also a river running between the Tree of Life and the Street of Gold. Its water was clear as crystal and sparkled like precious diamonds. It had no visible end as it flowed to its own tranquil music. I stood in the midst of all this heavenly beauty enjoying the glorious peace it offered until I was unfortunately awaken from this vision of the Throne of God.

Interpretation: Streets of Gold and Tree of Life

The Vision and The Promise

All you have seen in this vision are promises made to those who live Godly and labor for Me in this life. For all who hear the word of God say come let me take and drink from the water of life freely. Whosoever shall will endure to the end. I have stored up in My Kingdom an abundance of wealth, beauty and pleasure. The abundance of who I am is consumed and lies dormant in the glorious Tree of Life and the River of Living Water, until that day when the mystery shall be revealed. I have promised no more sickness, death, pain or sorrow. There will be joy forever more. My overcomers will be consumed in my glorious presence for eternity and there you will experience complete fullness in all things that surpasses all mortal imagination.

Bible reference

Revelation 22:1-3 - And he shewed me a pure river of water of life, clear as crystal, proceeding out of the throne of God and of the Lamb.

In the midst of the street of it, and on either side of the river, was the tree of life, which bare twelve manner of fruits, and yielded her fruit every month: and the leaves of the tree were for the healing of the nations.

And there shall be no more curse: but the throne of God and of the Lamb shall be in it; and his servants shall serve him:

The End Time

I was among a multitude of people climbing a huge rock. Everyone was racing with the intent to make it to the top. It was as if everyone was running away from something or someone. I looked behind me and saw a roaring ocean, moreover I saw that half of the sea was red like blood and was gradually moving closer to the rock. I noticed that the waves were intentionally trying to hit us from the rock, each force getting stronger and stronger. The forces of the waves were so powerful; some people were knocked from the rock to their death. Only those who held on with all their might were able to cling to the rock and endure the battering of the terrible waves. There were many who sustained and made it to the top of the rock.

As we walked, I saw a house to my left. I recognized it so I went inside to see what was going on. As I entered, I saw many people taking refuge there. Mothers and fathers with their children frantically searching through the bible while some knelt praying. I asked

36

someone what was going on. I was told there were many signs of the coming of the Lord.

Immediately as I walked outside, a lady tapped me on my shoulder and asked, "What can I do to be saved? I see all that is going on around me and I know Jesus is coming soon."

I answered her saying, "I perceive in my spirit that you know who Jesus is, but you need to accept Him as your Lord and Savior, repent of your sins and be baptized.

After a quick moment of hesitation she accepted Jesus into her heart and asked me to take her to a place where she could be baptized. In a nearby building I saw a multitude of people standing in line waiting their turn to be baptized. The lady joined the line and waited her turn. After a short time of waiting she came out rejoicing in the Spirit.

"It is done, I am covered by the blood of Jesus!" Still basking in the Spirit of God, we walked outside and to our surprise as we stepped from the side walk to the parking lot a life changing event happened. Suddenly the most inconceivable thing took place right before our eyes. The entire earth became pitch black. It was as if someone had turned off every power source of the entire world. Nothing was visible, no sun, moon or stars in the sky. It looked as if the sky had literally rolled away from existence. Amazingly, seen in its place was a glorious brightness from heaven, an indescribable appearance of the Glory of God. There was nowhere else to look but up to the sky. Everybody's attention was drawn to the sky awaiting the appearance of the Son of God.

Interpretation: The End Time

The Rock:

The Rock represents the Word of God. The Bible is the road map that will lead those who choose to follow Me back to where I Am. Without My Words sown deep in your hearts you will not survive the great day of sorrow and tribulation. Feed on My Words because it is the food of life.

Bible reference

Hebrew 4:12 - For the word of God is quick, and powerful, and sharper than any two-edged sword, piercing even to the dividing asunder of soul and spirit, and of the joints and marrow, and is a discerner of the thoughts and intents of the heart.

Luke 6:48 - He is like a man which built an house, and digged deep, and laid the foundation on a rock: and when the flood arose, the stream beat vehemently upon that house, and could not shake it: for it was founded upon a rock.

The Waves:

The waves are tests, temptations, turmoil and various types of tribulations that will come upon the earth before My return. Many Christians will be deceived, denouncing their faith in Me, while others will be deceivers, betraying their own brethren. Others will be distracted by the cares of this world, which will result in faithlessness in Me. But many will remember My Word and will hold Me to My promise. My Words will quicken you and give you strength in time of tribulation.

Bible reference

Matthew 24:21 - For then shall be great tribulation, such as was not seen since the beginning of the world to this time, no, nor ever shall be.

The Blood:

The blood signifies the many who will lose their lives during the great tribulation period and the spiritual death of those who will lose their faith in Me because of the cares of this life. It is happening presently because *My coming is closer than you think.*

Daniel 11:33 - And they that understand among the people shall instruct many: yet they shall fall by the sword, and by flame, by captivity, and by spoil, many days.

The House On The Rock:

The house upon the Rock represents the need for each person to establish a personal relationship with Me, through My Son, Jesus Christ. The stronger your relationship is with Me, the more spiritually strengthened you will be in the midst of your tribulations. I will strengthen you and faith will increase if you stand confident and have hope in My return.

Bible reference

2 Samuel 22:3 - The God of my rock; in him will I trust: he is my shield, and the horn of my salvation, my high tower, and my refuge, my savior, thou savest me from violence.

People Inside The House:

Everyone inside the house searched diligently and feverishly for refuge in the word of God. When you live your life according to My words your foundation will be firm and un-movable no matter what happens in your life. In the midst of tribulation you will find solace. A place to rest when My words are buried deep in your heart. Many will seek for the Word of Truth and shall not find it because there will be a famine of the Word.

Bible reference

Amos 8:11-12 - Behold, the days come, saith the Lord God, that I will send a famine in the land, not a famine of bread, nor athirst for water, but of hearing the words of the Lord. And they shall wander from sea to sea, and from the north even to the east, they shall run to and fro to seek the word of the Lord, and shall not find it.

The Darkness And The Light:

The sudden darkness that will appear signifies what shall take place prior to My return. The darkness represents the true and current state of the world, seen only through spiritual eyes. I will show you the truth about your reality, which is utter darkness (the temporal things seen with the naked eyes).

Everything in this world is temporal and simply an illusion. It will pass away. The true reality is spiritual, not temporal. I will prove it all to you by taking that which seem true to you and replace it with the only truth, which is Me. In the wink of an eye everything will melt away from the face of the earth and your attention will be drawn to the Truth. After I have taken that which belongs to Me, then I will set the stage for My appearance. I am the Lord, Your God, the Truth and the Life.

Bible reference

Matthew 24:29-30 - Immediately after the tribulation of those days shall the sun be darkened, and the moon shall not give her light, and the stars shall fall from heaven, and the powers of the heavens shall be shaken.

And then shall appear the sign of the Son of man in heaven: and then shall all the tribes of the earth mourn, and they shall see the Son of man coming in the clouds of heaven with power and great glory.

The End Time Tower of Babel

I found myself in a great tower with many different levels and people. There were no windows to the outside, just a glassed area overlooking the tower; a place called the pit of punishment. This pit had two parts: the first pit was covered with dirt and the second pit was an abyss of fire. There was a split in the center of the first level allowing you to see the inferno coming from the second level. Many people were whispering to each other saying that this place was where the antichrist housed all the Christians in order to force them into denouncing God. We were not allowed to talk about God, neither were we allowed to read the bible or pray. But somehow God allowed some of us to hide our bibles on our body.

We were separated at night to sleep in a small holding cell and at day we were taken to the glass area so we could witness other Christians as they were punished and killed. Even though officers constantly watched us, somehow God allowed us to talk with each other, pray and even read the bible when they were not paying attention.

Unfortunately, anyone found doing the things that were forbidden was taken to the pit of punishment. Many people were found guilty of disobeying the antichrist and was taken to the pit. The officers' job was not only to watch us, but also to punish those who were non-compliant with the rules of the tower. Some were forced into denouncing God by way of beatings, kicking and other means of torture. Ultimately, Christians were given the choice of denouncing God, or death. Some allowed fear to prevail and rejected Christ as their Savior, while others held on to their faith and was cast into the furnace.

47

Interpretation: The End Time Tower of Babel

The Tower:

The tower represents the kingdom of the antichrist that will be manifested according to My words at the appointed time. The existence of the tower demonstrates the control that he will have upon the entire world. I will give him power for a short time. He will persuade many to turn away from Me and deceive many into serving him instead. However, his primary purpose, according to My will is to be used as a strengthening tool for those who really trust and love Me. I promise that I will never leave you nor forsake you as you go through persecution for My namesake. Be strong and be of good courage.

Bible reference

Revelation 2:10 - Fear none of those things which thou shalt suffer: behold, the devil shall cast some of you into prison, that ye may be tried; and ye shall have tribulation ten days: be thou faithful unto death, and I will give thee a crown of life.

A Visit to Hell

I found myself in an old historic building. It was dark and depressing with no way out. The floors were old, the wall was stained with something resembling tar. There were various levels or floors to this building. I found myself running through the building from floor to floor. On each level I saw people lamenting as if they were being tormented by something. Some were laying on beds, others on the floor, still others were sitting in chairs and some walked around helplessly, they too were in severe pain.

When they saw me they began to call out for help. As I walked by them they were trying to touch me, but they were unable to reach. As I looked closer I could see the skin melting from their bodies, but then reappearing each time. It was as though there was an invisible fire removing their flesh from their bodies. It seemed as if the level of torment would increase by the intensity of their screams. There was great anguish in their voices. Some were yelling slurs of blasphemy against God, and some were begging the Lord for forgiveness.

The sound of pain and hopelessness was too much for me to bear. As I ran through the building I could feel the presence of a demonic force trying to trap me, but the presence of God allowed me to escape.

Interpretation: A Visit to Hell

The Holy Spirit told me I had visited hell. A place where no one wants to spend eternity. The presence of evil was everywhere. Each level in the building represents a different degree of torture. Some punishment was more severe than others, yet each person experiences punishment that will last forever. The punishment is continuous and nothing can stop the pain.

Some were calling out for help, but I couldn't help them even if it was a loved one or a friend, there was nothing I could do to ease their pain. The heat from the fire was intense. Their skin was melting like plastic in fire. Their screams were sounds of absolute torment and anguish. It was a surreal experience. Imagine, as soon as the skin melted, it would reappear only to start all over again and again forever. It was absolutely *horrible,* but *real!*

Bible reference

Revelation 21:8 - But the fearful, and unbeliever, and the abominable, and murderers, and whoremongers, and sorcerers, and idolaters and all liars, shall have their part in the lake *which burneth with fire and brimstone: which is the second death.*

Notes Of Inspiration To My Readers:

To all my brothers and sisters in Christ I greet you in the name of our soon coming King, *Jesus Christ*. It is an honor and a blessing from God to share these dreams that I so undeservedly received from Him. His instructions to me was for me to share them with others and to tell of His love and plans for us. He desires most to be united with His people, but we are not ready. Because of His endless love and mercy for us, He is granting us the chance to get ready for His entry. His vision for His people is that we would serve Him in spirit and in truth, keeping our eyes on things that are eternal and allowing Him alone to lead us. Be prayerful always, asking Him to keep us pure and spotless until the day of redemption.

All of these dreams have one thing in common, and that is, the fact that we are all on a spiritual journey to somewhere after this life. Where our journey leads us depends on the road we choose and the one we choose to follow.

For my readers who have not yet given their life to Jesus, I pray that something in this book will spark the need for a personal relationship with Him. The word of God says, *"And as it is appointed unto men once to die, but after this the judgment."* Hebrew 9:27.

After visiting hell and seeing the pain and torment on the faces of the people, I would not want anyone to spend eternity in such a place. You are the only one who can decide where your eternal life will be, heaven or hell.

Dear friends, let it not be hell. The fire cannot be quenched and the torment never stops. So let your choice be heaven for there you will be in paradise where there is peace and joy everlasting. Make Jesus your Lord and Savior. Live a life acceptable to Him and you will never experience the second death.

God told us that hell was made for Satan and his angels, not you and I. Just ask yourself these questions:

What if I die today? It could happen in a blink of an eye, in a car accident, heart attack; even in your sleep. We do not know when our time here on earth will come to an end.

Where will I spend my eternity, fire or paradise? You can choose now by saying this simple prayer from your heart.

Jesus, I am a sinner going to hell and I need You as my Savior. I can no longer rely on myself, my friends, or anything else. I need Your help to turn from my sinful life. This